A
MESSAGE TO
GARCIA

ELBERT HUBBARD (1856-1915)

A
MESSAGE TO
GARCIA

BY
ELBERT HUBBARD

APPLEWOOD BOOKS

A *Message to Garcia*
was originally published in 1899.
Applewood Books would like to thank
Paul A. McNulty for lending his copy of
A *Message to Garcia* for reproduction.

ISBN: 1-55709-200-1

Thank you for purchasing an Applewood Book.
Applewood reprints America's lively classics—books
from the past that are still of interest
to modern readers.
For a free copy of our current catalog, please write to
Applewood Books, Box 365, Bedford, MA 01730.

6 8 10 9 7

Library of Congress Cataloging-in-Publication Data
Hubbard, Elbert, 1856-1915.
    A message to Garcia : being a preachment / by Elbert Hubbard.—
Facsim. ed.
            p.   cm.
    Originally published: East Aurora, N.Y. : Roycrofters, 1899.
    ISBN 1-55709-200-1
    1. Success.   I. Title.
BJ1611.H8   1993
158'.1—dc20   92-40294
                                                CIP

APOLOGIA

HIS literary trifle, A MESSAGE TO GARCIA, was written one evening after supper, in a single hour. It was on the Twenty-second of February, Eighteen Hundred Ninety-nine, Washington's Birthday: we were just going to press with the March PHILISTINE ❧ ❧

The thing leaped hot from my heart, written after a trying day, when I had been endeavoring to train some rather delinquent

Hot from my heart

villagers to abjure the comatose state and get radioactive.

The immediate suggestion, though, came from a little argument over the teacups, when my boy Bert suggested that Rowan was the real hero of the Cuban War. Rowan had gone alone and done the thing—carried the message to Garcia.

It came to me like a flash! Yes, the boy is right, the hero is the man who does his work—who carries the message to Garcia. ❡ I got up from the table, and wrote A MESSAGE TO GARCIA. I thought so little of it that we ran it in the Magazine without a heading. The edition went out, and soon orders began to come

Yes, the boy is right

for extra copies of the March PHILISTINE, a dozen, fifty; a hundred, and when the American News Company ordered a thousand, I asked one of my helpers which article it was that stirred up the cosmic dust. "It's the stuff about Garcia," he said ✒ ✒

The next day a telegram came from George H. Daniels, of the New York Central Railroad thus, "Give price on one hundred thousand Rowan article in pamphlet form—Empire State Express advertisement on back —also how soon can ship."

I replied giving price, and stated we could supply the pamphlets in two years. Our facilities were

George H. Daniels orders

small and a hundred thousand booklets looked like an awful undertaking &•— &•—

The result was that I gave Mr. Daniels permission to reprint the article in his own way. He issued it in booklet form in editions of half a million. Two or three of these half-million lots were sent out by Mr. Daniels, and in addition the article was reprinted in over two hundred magazines and newspapers. It has been translated into all written languages.

At the time Mr. Daniels was distributing A MESSAGE TO GARCIA, Prince Hilakoff, Director of Russian Railways, was in this country. He was the

Three half-million lots

guest of the New York Central, and made a tour of the country under the personal direction of Mr. Daniels. The Prince saw the little book and was interested in it, more because Mr. Daniels was putting it out in big numbers, probably, than otherwise. ❡ In any event, when he got home he had the matter translated into Russian, and a copy of the booklet given to every railroad employee in Russia ❧ Other countries then took it up, and from Russia it passed into Germany, France, Spain, Turkey, Hindustan and China. During the war between Russia and Japan, every Russian soldier who went to the front was given a

Translated into Russian

copy of A MESSAGE TO GARCIA.

℃ The Japanese, finding the booklets in possession of the Russian prisoners, concluded it must be a good thing, and accordingly translated it into Japanese ֍ ֍

Translated into Japanese

And on an order of the Mikado, a copy was given to every man in the employ of the Japanese Government, soldier or civilian. ℃ Over forty million copies of A MESSAGE TO GARCIA have been printed. This is said to be a larger circulation than any other literary venture has ever attained during the lifetime of an author, in all history—thanks to a series of lucky accidents ֍

East Aurora,
December 1, 1913   E. H.

A MESSAGE TO GARCIA

I N all this Cuban business there is one man stands out on the horizon of my memory like Mars at perihelion.

When war broke out between Spain and the United States it was very necessary to communicate quickly with the leader of the Insurgents. Garcia was somewhere in the mountain fastnesses of Cuba—no one knew

The President needed a man

where ⚮ No mail or telegraph message could reach him. The President must secure his co-operation, and quickly.

What to do!

Some one said to the President, "There is a fellow by the name of Rowan will find Garcia for you, if anybody can."

And found one

Rowan was sent for and given a letter to be delivered to Garcia. How the "fellow by the name of Rowan" took the letter,

He delivered the message

sealed it up in an oilskin pouch, strapped it over his heart, in four days landed by night off the coast of Cuba from an open boat, disappeared into the jungle, and in three weeks came out on the other side of the Island, having traversed a hostile country on foot, and delivered his letter to Garcia—are things that I have no special desire now to tell in detail. The point that I wish to make is this: McKinley gave Rowan a letter to be delivered to Garcia; Rowan took the letter and did not ask, "Where is he at?"

By the Eternal! there is a man whose form should be cast in deathless bronze and the statue placed in every college of the land. It is not book-learning young men need, nor instruction about this, and that, but a stiffening of the vertebrae which will cause them to be loyal to a trust, to act promptly, concen-

The Moral

trate their energies : do the thing —"Carry a message to Garcia." ✿ ✿

There are
other Garcias

General Garcia is dead now, but there are other Garcias. No man who has endeavored to carry out an enterprise where many hands were needed, but has been well-nigh appalled at times by the imbecility of the average man — the inability or unwillingness to concentrate on a thing and do it.

Slipshod assistance, foolish inattention, dowdy indifference, and half-hearted work seem the rule; and no man succeeds, unless by hook or crook or threat he forces or bribes other men to assist him; or mayhap, God in His goodness performs a miracle, and sends him an Angel of Light for an assistant.

You, reader, put this matter to a test: You are sitting now in your office—six clerks are within call. Summon any one and make this request: "Please look in the encyclopedia and make a brief memorandum for me concerning the life of Correggio." Will the clerk quietly say, "Yes, sir," and go do the task?

On your life he will not. He will look at you out of a fishy eye and ask one or more of the following questions:

Who was he?

Which encyclopedia?

Where is the encyclopedia?

Where is the encyclopedia?

Was I hired for that?

Don't you mean Bismarck?

What's the matter with Charlie doing it?

Is he dead?

Is there any hurry?

Sha'n't I bring you the book and let you look it up yourself?

What do you want to know for?

And I will lay you ten to one that after you have answered the questions, and explained how to find the information, and why you want it, the clerk will go off and get one of the other clerks to help him try to find Garcia — and then come back and tell you there is no such man. Of course I may lose my bet, but according to the

What's the matter with Charlie doing it?

I wasn't hired for that anyway!

Law of Average I will not ❧
Now, if you are wise, you will
not bother to explain to your
"assistant" that Correggio is
indexed under the C's, not in the
K's, but you will smile very
sweetly and say "Never mind,"
and go look it up yourself. And
this incapacity for independent
action, this moral stupidity, this
infirmity of the will, this unwillingness to cheerfully catch hold
and lift—these are the things
that put pure Socialism so far
into the future. If men will not
act for themselves, what will
they do when the benefit of
their effort is for all?

A first mate with knotted club
seems necessary; and the dread

Catch
hold
and lift

of getting "the bounce" Satur-
day night holds many a worker
to his place. Advertise for a
stenographer, and nine out of
ten who apply can neither spell
nor punctuate — and do not
think it necessary to.

Can such a one write a letter
to Garcia?

"You see that bookkeeper,"
said the foreman to me in a
large factory.

"Yes; what about him?"

Who wants
a man like
this?

"Well, he's a fine accountant,
but if I'd send him up town on
an errand, he might accomplish
the errand all right, and on the
other hand, might stop at four
saloons on the way, and when
he got to Main Street would for-

get what he had been sent for."

❦ Can such a man be entrusted to carry a message to Garcia? ❧ We have recently been hearing much maudlin sympathy expressed for the "downtrodden denizens of the sweatshop" and the "homeless wanderer searching for honest employment," and with it all often go many hard words for the men in power ❧ Nothing is said about the employer who grows old before his time in a vain attempt to get frowsy ne'er-do-wells to do intelligent work; and his long, patient striving after "help" that does nothing but loaf when his back is turned ❧ In every store and factory there is a con-

The weeding-out process

stant weeding-out process going on. The employer is constantly sending away "help" that have shown their incapacity to further the interests of the business, and others are being taken on. No matter how good times are, this sorting continues: only, if times are hard and work is scarce, the sorting is done finer —but out and forever out the incompetent and unworthy go. It is the survival of the fittest. Self-interest prompts every employer to keep the best — those who can carry a message to Garcia ❧ ❧

I know one man of really brilliant parts who has not the ability to manage a business of his own, and yet who is absolutely worthless to any one else, because he carries with him constantly the insane suspicion that his employer is oppressing, or intending to oppress, him. He can not give orders, and he will not receive them. Should a message be given him to take to Garcia, his answer would probably be, "Take it yourself!" ✒ Tonight this man walks the streets looking for work, the wind whistling through his threadbare coat. No one who knows him dare employ him, for he is a regular firebrand of discontent. He is impervious to reason, and the only thing that can impress him is the toe of a thick-soled Number Nine boot.

€ Of course I know that one so morally deformed is no less to be pitied than a physical cripple; but in our pitying let us drop a tear, too, for the men who are striving to carry on a great enterprise, whose working hours are not limited by the whistle, and whose hair is fast turning white through the struggle to hold in line dowdy indifference, slipshod imbecility, and the heartless ingratitude which, but for their enterprise, would be both hungry and homeless.

A physical cripple

Have I put the matter too strongly? Possibly I have; but when all the world has gone a-slumming I wish to speak a word of sympathy for the man who succeeds—the man who, against great odds, has directed the efforts of others, and having succeeded, finds there's nothing in it: nothing but bare board and clothes. I have carried a dinner-pail and worked for day's wages, and I have also been an employer of labor, and I know there is something to be said on both sides. There is no excellence, per se, in poverty; rags are no recommendation; and all employers are not rapacious and high-handed, any more than all poor men are virtuous. My heart goes out to the man who does his work when the "boss" is away, as well as when he is at

A word
of sympathy
for the man
who succeeds

Rags not
necessarily a
recommendation

home. And the man who, when given a letter for Garcia, quietly takes the missive, without asking any idiotic questions, and with no lurking intention of chucking it into the nearest sewer, or of doing aught else but deliver it, never gets "laid off" nor has to go on a strike for higher wages. Civilization is one long, anxious search for just such individuals. Anything such a man asks shall be granted. He is wanted in every city, town and village—in every office, shop, store and factory. The world cries out for such; he is needed and needed badly — the man who can "Carry a Message to Garcia." ❧ ❧

Twenty-two

Good men are always needed

Needed today and needed badly— a man!